This is SAN FRANCISCO

THE UPS, DOWNS, INS, AND OUTS OF THE CITY BY THE BAY

Alexander Barrett

Microcosm Publishing
Portland, Ore

This is San Francisco
THE UPS, DOWN, INS, AND OUTS OF THE CITY BY THE BAY

© Alexander Barrett, 2019
This edition © Microcosm Publishing 2019
First published September 10, 2019

ISBN 978-1-62106-812-9
This is Microcosm #266

To join the ranks of high-class stores that feature Microcosm titles, talk to your local rep: In the U.S. **Como** (Atlantic), **Fujii** (Midwest), **Book Travelers West** (Pacific), **Turnaround** in Europe, **UTP/Manda** in Canada, **New South** in Australia, and **Baker & Taylor GPS** in Asia, Africa, India, and other countries.

For a catalog, write or visit:
Microcosm Publishing
2752 N Williams Ave.
Portland, OR 97227
www.Microcosm.Pub

Library of Congress Cataloging-in-Publication Data

Names: Barrett, Alexander, 1983- author.
Title: This is San Francisco : the ups, downs, ins, and outs of the City by the Bay / Alexander Barrett.
Description: Portland, OR : Microcosm Publishing, 2019. | Description based on print version record and CIP data provided by publisher; resource not viewed.
Identifiers: LCCN 2019013237 (print) | LCCN 2019014577 (ebook) | ISBN 9781621065869 (e-book) | ISBN 9781621068129 (pbk.)
Subjects: LCSH: San Francisco (Calif.)--Description and travel.
Classification: LCC F869.S34 (ebook) | LCC F869.S34 B37 2019 (print) | DDC 917.94/6104--dc23
LC record available at https://lccn.loc.gov/2019013237

By the time I landed, it was the past.

The flight was eleven hours long, but thanks to the international date line, we arrived four hours before we departed. These were hours I had lived before in the hot, humanity-filled streets of Shanghai, where it seemed that everyone's elbow was trying to connect with my stomach and everyone's spit was doing its best to land on my shoes. I told myself I wouldn't miss this place as I got into a cab and raced to the airport.

At the same moment, I stepped out of a cab in San Francisco and was greeted with quiet. The cloud cover was low and lazy. The streets were the opposite of bustling. And as I watched a group of dogs calmly congregating in a nearby park, a hummingbird took a break from its incessant flapping, landed on the fence next to me, and hung out for a while.

In its jet-lagged stupor, my body was deeply confused. It cried out to be elbowed and spit on. I needed more bustle. I had come back to my home country to relax after a few years of extreme work and travel, but this was insanity. I collapsed into bed knowing that I should have never messed with the space-time continuum.

I woke up before dawn. The sky over the East Bay went from a deep purple to a pinkish orange. The sun hit Potrero Hill, then bounced over to Dolores Park, illuminating the dewed glass backboards of the basketball court. The last remaining fog acknowledged defeat and went wherever fog goes when it's not time to be foggy. I could see Pacific Heights, Bernal Heights, and all the Heights in between. The houses were a breathtaking mishmash of pastels. Somewhere in the distance, a car horn sounded quickly and quietly as if to say, "I really hate to bother you, but if you'd set your phone down for just a moment, you'll see that the light is green and we can both be on our way to yoga class."

At that moment, I didn't need the spit and elbows. The desire for bustle faded away and was replaced by whatever it is that San Francisco does. And whatever it is that San Francisco is.

It's now three years later. Since that moment, I've

gotten to know this city. I've explored its ups and downs, easts and wests, its humble beauty and its ridiculous idiosyncrasies.

This is a guidebook, but it won't tell you what to see or where to eat. Actually, maybe a little of each, I'm not sure yet. Anyway, that's not really the point. This book is a guide to all the specific little things that make San Francisco, San Francisco. It's a compendium of the sights, sounds, and moments that give this city its unmistakable feeling.

Ready?

This is San Francisco.

the Palette

San Francisco's color palette is diverse just like the people who live here. Most of it is slightly muted, but that really doesn't describe these people at all.

Every morning and evening the sky becomes a sea of pink and orange, captivating everyone within view and stopping commuters dead in their tracks.

All year round, the floral blooms bring bold reds and purples to the city's stoops and windowsills.

And then there are the buildings. Sure there are plain white houses and crazy neon houses, regular brick houses and houses covered with portraits of every animal in the jungle, but for the most part, the city is covered with gentle hues. Soothing yellows, approachable pinks, unexpected reds, blues both sky and midnight, surprisingly okay browns, and greens that seem to disappear into the surrounding succulents.

The best part is that homes of the same color are rarely positioned next to each other. When you look at the city from one of its many peaks, the vista, perhaps diffused by a layer of fog, blends into a stunning tapestry suitable for any baby's blanket or modern art fan's wall.

As you read, you'll find a few of my other favorite San Francisco colors. If you flip the pages really fast, you might even begin to see what it's like to stand at the top of Corona Heights Park on a sunny day and gaze out over the city.

Kinda.

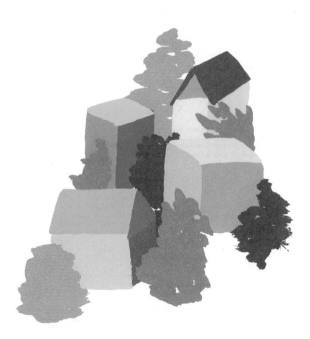

Say you're in Manhattan and you are straight-up freaking out.

You need to escape. You need to get away from the concrete and the noise. You need to be somewhere soothing and pastoral. You need to be somewhere green.

Well, Central Park is just about the only place you can completely fill your field of vision with natural beauty. You'd better jump into a cab and start your deep breathing exercises.

Now say you're in San Francisco and you're having the same issue.

Don't worry, you're good.

You can go to Mount Davidson, Fort Funston, Twin Peaks, Stern Grove, Glen Canyon, Forest Knolls, Buena Vista Park, Bernal Heights, Land's End and probably a few dozen others.

Oh, and you should probably go to Golden Gate Park, which is of a similar shape to Central Park, only bigger. And if none of those interest you, walk on up to the Presidio, which is even bigger.

For a place with such a limited amount of housing, you'd think somebody would have paved over all this beautiful green space and put up high-rises. But this city knows better.

I'm not going to pretend that San Francisco can't be a stressful place. It has the same struggles as any other city. It has traffic, noise, high-powered business deals, crime, and subways that don't want to move when you really, really need them to move.

In Manhattan, that energy bounces around the streets and echoes off every building, creating a cacophony of stress that gives the city a certain feeling. It's fast-walkin', horn-honkin', and big-talkin'.

But here, that energy rolls down the hills, shimmies around a cable car or two, then eventually finds its way into a nice eucalyptus grove and gets lost. Things slow down and worries fade. Inner-city pressure can get you down, but all you have to do is walk a few blocks and suddenly you're not in a city anymore. You are simply one small part of this beautiful, natural world. Then you can hug a nice tree, convene with a friendly squirrel, and you're back to normal.

I'm not saying that green space makes San Francisco a better city than New York, I'm just saying that if a gentle breeze through some big trees has become more exciting than bright lights and late nights, this might be the place for you.

A few party people sit on the benches along 20th Street with their half-full forties, watching the sunrise and trying to make Friday night last forever. Their extended evening is eventually brought to a close by the whistle of a nearby high-intensity boot camp class. They shuffle off to some bed somewhere as fitness ensues.

Before the boot camp can finish their squats, the dogs and their owners take control of the green space. The statue of Miguel Hidalgo, the father of Mexican independence, slowly smiles as the sunlight washes over him. He oversees every session of fetch and tries to enjoy the new graffiti that an average Friday night in San Francisco has bestowed upon him. In these few quiet moments, he prepares himself. Because it is officially Saturday in Dolores Park. And the circus is about to begin.

Around ten o'clock, minivans exploding with harried parents and party decorations pull up to the curb in front of the picnic area. They gotta get this show on the road before their child's birthday is engulfed in weed smoke and exposed back tattoos.

The morning people show up next. Armed with prosecco, orange juice, and blankets, they stake their claim early. A nice spot with a view of the city. Anywhere that isn't wet. The blankets go down, the mimosa flows and they wait. When their sleeping friends finally get it together and show up, the morning people will be heralded as heroes.

As the morning mist burns away, the others arrive. They bring guitars, blow-up couches, portable gazebos, and six-packs upon six-packs. If the clouds cooperate and the sun is out, the park will be full of humanity by two in the afternoon.

Welcome to Dolores Park Beach. It's a collection of cocktail parties disguised as a day spent in nature. Blaring boom boxes next to the silent yoga mats. The possibility of new love blossoming in line for the public restroom. It is both a scene and every scene existing in perfect harmony.

The six-packs help, but so does the hyperlocal economy. Sure, there are ice cream carts rolling around, but there are also a few guys with boxes of coconuts and handles of rum. Open one with a machete and pour a little of the other inside and everyone is doing just fine. Then there are the pot purveyors. Nice people with wicker baskets full of anything you could ever think to smoke or eat.

But the king of Dolores Park is the Truffle Man, a gentleman with a delightful straw hat subtly shaped like a pineapple selling weed truffles out of several lovely copper pots, each with its own flavor and topped by a tiny umbrella to keep everything cool. This is no seedy operation. It's a mellow public service with a smile that adds an extra layer of ridiculousness to the proceedings. I've heard the Truffle Man might be leaving the park and taking his business to the dispensaries. If that's true, I wish him well. The park will miss him, especially those who end up buying one of those massive weed Rice Krispies Treats and end up in a ball of giggles all day.

On my first weekend in San Francisco, I stepped out of my apartment ready for a quiet Saturday afternoon of reading in my local park, but instead walked straight into this daytime quasi-rave. I walked around awhile and took in the sights. After failing to find a single square of grass to park on, I headed back to my building and ran into a neighbor who was on his way to meet friends.

"Well, it's crowded out there. Don't they know there's beach a few miles from here?" I asked.

"Yeah, but not one with sun," he replied.

That's it. They're here for the sun. It's a precious commodity in a city with beaches that are either covered with fog or in a perpetual windstorm. Dolores Park is the closest thing to a beach San Francisco has for the huddled masses yearning to be tan.

The only thing missing is the ocean. But who needs the ocean when you have that skyline?

By four o'clock, the fog begins to crawl over Twin Peaks. Blankets are rolled, inflatable couches deflated, and the gazebos toppled once more. Sunglasses are tucked away as minds turn from drinks to dinner.

The beach empties and the park returns. Only for a few hours, though. Tomorrow is Sunday. And Sunday is another beach day.

Before we begin, let's all take a healthy step back from the idea that it's totally normal to have a federal penitentiary just off the coast and in plain view of a major American city.

Little weird, huh?

Seems like it would have been fine to leave it to the birds who called the island home for hundreds of years. It also would have been fine to call it quits after somebody bought it and put up the very first lighthouse on the West Coast. What a lovely thing to gaze upon as you watch the sun disappear into the Pacific.

But no.

Couldn't they have made it just a regular jail? You know, full of affable drunks and altruistic pickpockets?

Nope. It had to be the home of the prisoners who were too dangerous to be contained at their local prisons. Just the worst people.

Well, it was only a federal penitentiary for about thirty years; surely after it closed they could have made something nice out of that land, right? Like a fun bird sanctuary or a beach you can only reach via kayak or something?

Nah, we'll just preserve it as it was and offer tours so people can experience firsthand the torturous conditions in which the worst people in America lived for that short period of time.

Really?

Tourists will love it.

Huh. Okay.

Alcatraz has become the Pirates of the Caribbean to San Francisco's Disneyland. The part that feels a little secret and dangerous, but is actually just a nice place to spend an afternoon.

It reminds us that even lovely, pleasant cities have a dark side. And we all love to take a dip into the dark side every once in a while.

Especially if the dark side is home to so many wonderful birds, seals, and views.

Wow, did they really give prisoners with life sentences an unobstructed view of one of the most beautiful cities in America? Seems a little unusual.

And cruel!

the Parrots

If you're a tourist in San Francisco and you want to see the sights, you'll probably end up somewhere east of Van Ness Avenue and north of Market Street. That's where most of the stuff you've heard of is. And all the shopping. It's the part of the city that feels like a city. It has lots of foot traffic, lots of people trying to hand you lots of flyers, and lots of commotion.

Honestly, it's not my favorite place to be. And that says a lot about the rest of San Francisco because east of Van Ness and north of Market is full of stunning vistas, lovely residential neighborhoods, and the best Chinatown outside of actual China.

But sometimes, when I have to go to the dentist or do some worky work out of a unfamiliar office, I have to be there. And as lovely and painless as it is to see Susie Shin, DDS, and as much as I enjoy being gainfully employed, this place never puts me in the best mood.

That was until the day I'd been cooped up in a room all day while the sun was busy shining outside. I was cranky. I needed coffee. Brad, Tyler and I went outside and headed for Union Square. I saw a flock of birds flying overhead, but didn't pay them any attention. We were on a mission.

That's when they started talking.

It was a kind of chatter I had never heard before. It wasn't a classic honk or an obnoxious caw. It was a conversation. It stopped me in my tracks. I looked up and asked Tyler what was going on.

"Parrots."

A flock of feral parrots living downtown. On Telegraph Hill, to be exact. The offspring of escaped or released pets.

This is what San Francisco does best. It gives you everything you'd expect from a major city and then it gives you a little twist. You'd expect tall buildings and crowded sidewalks to be paired with a pigeon or several hundred. But no. Parrots. Not a dingy gray, but bright green and red. Not urban, but tropical. I was transported. I went on vacation for the thirty or so seconds they stayed in my line of sight.

All of a sudden, east of Van Ness and north of Market was just as magical as the rest of the city. My bad mood disappeared.

And the coffee was incredible.

Sutro Baths

In 1896, former mayor and local badass, Adolph Sutro, opened a palace of bathing. An oasis where the people of San Francisco could soak away their worries in the saltwater of the Pacific Ocean without all that "being outside" nonsense.

The largest indoor swimming facility in the world, it was a glass cathedral to relaxation, and in the 1960s, it burned to the ground (some say for the insurance money).

Its remains are still there in the little inlet just north of Cliff House and just south of Land's End. If you walk down, you can climb over the twisted metal and broken concrete of its foundation. You can disappear into its caves and poke your head into forgotten, darkened pools. These are San Francisco's modern ruins. A window into the not-quite-so-distant past.

It's a little like touring the ruins of Greece, but instead of seeing the remains of a temple dedicated to a beloved goddess, you see the remains of a temple dedicated to chilling out.

Instead of visiting the birthplace of democracy, you visit a place where some people once had a nice Saturday afternoon.

And you are probably having one, too.

Just look at the two of you.

You are adorable.

You're on a romantic stroll somewhere in the city. You don't really care where. You sneak glances into each other's eyes. You pull each other close as you turn a corner to head home and a monolith appears before you.

This is a hill.

One of those classic San Francisco hills you've heard about. But now that you're staring it in the face, you understand why you've heard about it. It's too steep. It's too high. And it is standing between you and a wonderful evening.

You laugh at the hill. "It's just a hill," you say to each other. "We are two physically capable humans. We can do this."

And so you begin your ascent. The first twenty feet are fine. You are both happy in the knowledge that you have chosen to mate with a physically fit, adventurous human, just like you.

Then the incline increases. You let go of each other's hands. You half smile as if to say, "I can do this, I just need full range of motion." Your smiles fade as you try to keep your heavy breathing inconspicuous.

Your breathing deepens as you lose track of each other. You turn around to see if walking backward helps.

It doesn't.

Now it's a competition. Maybe it's a little sexy at first. Who is going to come out on top? You might laugh about this.

But sexiness quickly gives way to muscle fatigue and you turn into two piles of steaming flesh splayed out on the sidewalk.

Your muscles cramp. The wind whips away what little life remained in your bodies.And you cannot go on. Unless one of you finds some kind of sustenance. As night falls, you turn to each other knowing that one of you has to make the ultimate sacrifice if the other is to go on.

You hold each other close.

You cry.

You wonder how yet another date in this city has ended in cannibalism.

Then you remember that San Francisco has a robust public transportation system and there's a bus coming that would love to take you up and over that hill.

You accept defeat, get on the bus, and spend the rest of the night trying to forgive each other.

the Golden Gate Bridge

I wonder how all the other landmarks felt when Golden Gate Bridge opened to traffic in 1937.

Was Golden Gate Park excited that it would have a new friend to hang out with?

Were the cable cars relieved that they finally had another luminary of transportation with which to share their deepest secrets?

Did Coit Tower look over from its perch on Telegraph Hill and say, "Well, hello. I notice you're art deco. I'm art deco, too. When do you get off work?"

Did any of them realize that they were about to become second-class tourist destinations, forever trapped in the shadow of this steel gargantua?

This chapter is obligatory. If you have ever heard of San Francisco, you know there's a big orange bridge here.

It's the most photographed bridge in the world. It's featured prominently in every physical representation

of civic pride in the city. You'll see it in countless murals in the Mission and on a heap of tee shirts in Chinatown.

There's a reason the Giants' logo is orange.

Everything that needs to be said about the Golden Gate has already been said. But there's one incredible thing about it that struck me after years of living here: it doesn't get old.

I don't mind seeing the bridge in murals or on shirts. I always get a tingly feeling when I walk to the top of Twin Peaks and see it peeking out from behind the Presidio. Last weekend, I went kayaking in the bay and watched the sunset behind those massive suspension cables. My body wasn't quite sure what to do with that level of beauty.

There's something about its scale that makes you feel both small and safe. And there's something about that exact shade of orange that makes the bridge feel playful. Like maybe it wasn't really built to solve the problem of getting people from San Francisco to Marin County without putting their car on a boat. Maybe they put it there just to make you feel good.

Even though I've driven across it countless times, I feel like a kid every time I go under those two towers. And

I still crane my neck to keep my eyes on them as long as I possibly can.

There's a reason that the Golden Gate Bridge is the most recognizable part of the city.

I hope the other landmarks can learn to accept that one day.

the Bay Bridge

Poor Bay Bridge.

All it wants is to be as cool as its sibling to the west.

And it tries so hard.

Instead of being just one regular bridge, the Bay Bridge is really two bridges. The western half has a classic suspension bridge motif going on. As you pass over, its calming blue/green/gray paint job eases you into the vibe of San Francisco. The eastern half has more of a forward-thinking design. This section was opened in 2013 as a replacement for the original section, which wasn't the most attractive bridge you've ever seen, if I'm honest. Now when you walk, bike, or drive across, it feels as if you're travelling into a minimalist fantasyland.

Need a break from the monotony of your daily bridge crossing? Well, you're in luck, because the two sections of the Bay Bridge meet at not one but two islands. Both Yerba Buena Island and the man-made Treasure Island are accessible via exits in both directions. Here, you can take in stunning views of the city, take a hike through the hills, or even go wine tasting, which seems a little dicey because you drove here, remember? Don't forget to hydrate.

If that weren't enough to make this the most popular bridge in the Bay, the eastern section features a nightly light show by artist Leo Villareal that has been a mainstay since 2013.

But no matter what the Bay Bridge does for the people of the Bay Area, it will never be San Francisco's "golden" child. It's just not iconic enough.

It's sad. But at least it can take solace in the fact that it gets double the amount of people to their destination everyday than that other bridge.

Gold Space

Depending on the time of year and amount of rainfall, some of San Francisco's green spaces may dry out and turn into gold spaces.

They will be just as lovely and revitalizing.

Burritos

Since the 60s, San Francisco has been on a quest to either create or discover the best Mission-style burrito.

Unlike its counterparts in other areas of California, the Mission-style burrito is filled as full as its stretchy, steamed flour tortilla will allow. Rice takes up most of the space, but beans and salsa do their part, too. Of course, if you make your burrito "Super," cheese, sour cream, and guacamole will join the party and give you the most satisfying stomachache of your life.

Many restaurants claim to be birthplace of the Mission-style burrito. Some of them even have that claim painted across the front of their building. No matter which place you choose, you'll see a collection of plaques from various publications from various years announcing that at least at one point, this establishment was the home of the best Mission-style burrito.

If you ask the locals, you'll get a very different and definitive answer from everyone. Some are loyal to their neighborhood spot. Others think you should go to one place for the carne asada, another place for the chicken, and a third if you want to mix them together. And there's always one guy who knows about this hole in the wall with the best carnitas. It's two hours away, but if you're driving, he'd be happy to show you.

It's a lot to take in. After taking in all this information, you feel confused and sad and alone and you don't know where to go and maybe you just want to eat a salad instead. Well, don't worry. I've tried just about every burrito in the Mission and I have finally discovered the answer to this decades-long dilemma.

The best burrito in San Francisco is the one currently making its way into your face.

If you go to any of the burrito places in the Mission, you will not walk out with a bad burrito, you will walk out with a little bundle of joy. A collection of ingredients developed over generations, contained in an edible, just-north-of-mouth-sized sheath. Congratulations, you are about to experience unadulterated happiness.

When you take your first bite, you should have a mouthful representative of the burrito as a whole. The tortilla seems to melt away on your tongue, eagerly allowing access to the treasure within. The beans are first to arrive. They've been cooking away all day, just waiting to unleash their sweet earthiness on a willing victim. Their attack is followed closely by the reassuring silkiness of the guacamole, letting you know that it was okay to spend that extra couple bucks on a Super Burrito because avocado's acids are not only fatty, they are also essential. As you let that soak in, the sour cream rushes in screaming, "I MAY NOT BE ESSENTIAL, BUT I'M GONNA MAKE YOUR TONGUE FEEL GOOOOD!" At this point, you may begin to question your food decision-making abilities. Clearly, this sleeping bag full of calories is too rich for your blood. But then, in the nick of time, the salsa cuts through your inner turmoil like a knife with its freshness and acidity. The full package. One perfect mouthful.

And then of course, as if you weren't completely full already, the rice brings up the rear.

Now, if you take a bite of a burrito and your first thought is, "I wonder if this could have been better," you have to take a good hard look at your priorities. There are plenty of things in this life that require careful contemplation and analysis, but a burrito—especially a burrito from San Francisco—is not one of them. There's a burrito in San Diego called the "California Burrito." It contains french fries. That's a burrito we should think twice about before inhaling. But up here, stop worrying.

By applying some kind of value system to these beautiful creations, you are missing the point.

There is a force in the universe that wants us to have the Mission-style burrito. And it doesn't want us to talk about them. It wants us to sit down on a bench, tear through a mess of foil, and achieve enlightenment.

Taqueria Cancun

⭐⭐⭐⭐⭐

Pancho Villa Taqueria

⭐⭐⭐⭐⭐

Taqueria El Farolito

⭐⭐⭐⭐⭐

La Taqueria

⭐⭐⭐⭐⭐

Taqueria El Buen Sabor

⭐⭐⭐⭐⭐

Taqueria La Cumbre

⭐⭐⭐⭐⭐

El Metate

★★★★★

La Palma Mexicatessen

★★★★★

Taqueria San Francisco

★★★★★

El Toro Taqueria

★★★★★

Papalote Mexican Grill

★★★★★

Taqueria El Castillo

★★★★★

Every spring, a turf war breaks out on San Francisco's streets.

It's a floral fracas. A botanical brawl. An inharmonious hassle for horticultural hierarchy.

In one corner, the California Poppy (*Eschscholzia californica*). There's a reason this little champion became the state flower of California. Humble in its beauty and confident in its simplicity, it grows with a gentle ruggedness just about wherever it wants. Even when California experiences drought conditions, this Poppy shows up to keep the population smiling.

In the other corner, Nasturtium (*Tropaeolum majus*). While this flower grows just as easily as its adversary, it is not content to simply take its place in San Francisco's backdrop. The Nasturtium grandstands with its slim, dainty stem and its perfect, almost ceramic round leaves. It knows it looks good and it definitely thinks it's better than you. The Nasturtium understands that people will always keep it around because every single part of it is edible. Its leaves add a peppery note to any salad, and its petals add color and mystique to any upscale pastry.

Little does it know that the Poppy is edible, too. Sure, it might not sustain you if you happen to get lost in Golden Gate Park for weeks at a time, but it will mildly sedate you, so you might not care as much about your impending doom.

The California Poppy can be found everywhere. In small gardens, along your favorite urban hiking trail, even growing between the cracks of the sidewalks. But the Nasturtium is amassing its forces. Visit Stern Grove in the Outer Sunset, for example. Hiding inside are vast slopes of Nasturtium, sitting quietly in the dappled sunlight, planning their attack.

As the battle between these behemoths rages all summer, they turn the city's green spaces into fields of orange, bringing to mind the Golden Gate Bridge after a fresh coat of paint.

But every year, before a victor can be determined, the season ends, the fog rolls back in, and the petals fall.

These flowers rest for the winter, saving their strength for the struggle ahead.

Maybe a winner will never be crowned, but the battle adds one more incredible swatch to San Francisco's already vibrant palette.

Sea Lions

Just off Pier 39 is a collection of floating docks that are home to a mess of big ol' sea lions.

People show up in droves to lean against the railing and watch them. They watch them sleep. They watch them get some sun. They watch them jump into the water. They watch them sleep again. And they take pictures.

Then they put their cameras down and think, "Hmm. I like sleeping. I like getting some sun. I like jumping into the water. Why isn't this my life?"

They wonder where humanity went wrong. Why do we have to look at these phones and drive these cars and be slaves to this money when there are places to lie down in the sun?

They imagine themselves ripping off all their clothes, jumping into the bay, and starting a new life as a marine mammal.

For a moment, their worries disappear. They close

their eyes and smile as they focus on the warmth of the sun on their face.

Then, as they breathe deep the sea air, they get a whiff of that classic sea lion rotting fish stench and immediately come back to reality.

Maybe this isn't such a perfect fantasy after all.

Before we get into the nitty-gritty of these giants of public transportation, let's pause to consider their names.

BART.

Muni.

They're fun to say. BART sounds like the punchline to a joke no one told. It's quick, it's sharp, but it has that goofy ol' B up front to make you smile. Muni has "mew," so I'm already thinking about cats and I'm already happy. Tack on an "eeee" sound and the word ascends to a level of cuteness no public transportation system has ever reached before. In an unimaginative world filled with subways and metros, these two names tell the world that this city is ready to get weird.

Much like its name, BART is pretty no-nonsense for the most part. It has five heavy rail lines and it was, until recently, the home of some of the funkiest-looking and -smelling upholstered seats I've ever seen. It felt like a disused movie theater from the seventies in there. Don't worry, they've switched out the upholstery for easier-to-clean materials.

BART can take you from Millbrae to many destinations in the deep East Bay. But they'll only take you to eight places in the city itself: Balboa Park, Glen Park, 24th Street/Mission, 16th Street/Mission, Civic Center, Powell Street, Montgomery Street, and Embarcadero.

Every line that goes through the city makes all of these stops. A straight shot underneath Mission Street, Market Street, then under the bay to Oakland. It's almost as if BART's designers spent all of their time on this one strip of San Francisco. "It's great here! No one is going to want to go anywhere else; let's just make all the trains go to this one street and call it a day."

Unfortunately, a lot of people would rather be anywhere other than Market Street. It's the part of San Francisco that feels like it could be any city. Just as long as you're not looking directly at the magnificent Ferry Building at the edge of the bay.

That's where Muni comes in. Muni is BART's overachieving cousin.

We're going to have busses, of course, but I really think we can do better. I think we can get people where they need to go and give them a unique experience at the same time. Here me out: light rail. We all love trains, but what if they're lighter? It feels European. It feels premium. You know what we should do? On one of those routes, we should run exclusively old-timey streetcars from around the globe. This is a classy city and our public transportation needs to reflect that.

Muni picks up where…

HOLD ON, almost forgot: cable cars! RIGHT!? Classic SF. Okay, that's good for now, but don't be surprised if there's more because I'm thinking monorail, I'm thinking gondola, I'm thinking submarines, who knows?

Muni picks up where BART leaves off. It'll get you wherever you need to go within city limits. It may take a while, but that's okay, because there's one thing Muni has that BART does not: charm.

Its logo is a classic. Reminiscent of San Francisco's hilly terrain, a psychedelic blacklight poster, and the NASA logo that also came out in 1975. The SFMTA wanted to be prepared for a future in which there would be flying streetcars. Also a future in which the combination of orange, brown, and maroon would never go out of style. It might look slightly dated but it has become a much loved element of San Francisco's visual lexicon. If they try to change it, there will be protests.

There's something romantic about a streetcar. It's the same for a cable car, actually, but we'll get to that later. I like to sit at the top of Dolores Park in the early evening. The sky is a deep blue peppered with pink clouds. The grass is a dark green sprinkled with blankets of all colors. Then, suddenly, the two are bisected by the arrival of a northbound J-Church streetcar. A *deus ex machina* delivering both audio/visual stimulation and perhaps some new friends to hang out with. It is truly a magical moment.

And then there are the historic carriages. Candy-colored bits of anachronism to upend your expectations for the day. There's even an open-air car called the Boat Tram. It doesn't normally run, but you can rent it out for parties or journeys of self-discovery. You can rent out any car that runs on Muni, actually.

I only know this because one day as I walked to my car, the Boat Tram emerged from the Muni passageway next to Church Street. I had never seen an open-air car before, and from the party going on inside, it looked like a pretty good place to be. As I stood there waiting for it to pass, a gentleman on the tram looked at me and said, "Hey! You want a Jell-O shot?"

It just so happened that I did.

At the corner of 20th Street and Church Street stands a golden fire hydrant. It was the only hydrant to stay connected to water during the earthquake of 1906 and it's the only reason the Mission District is still standing. It saved countless lives, homes, and businesses. Every year on the anniversary of the quake, people leave flowers to pay tribute to its achievement.

Near the intersection of 45th Avenue and Sloat Boulevard in the Outer Sunset stands a large bust of a dapper dachshund wearing a chef's hat. He is there to pay tribute to Doggie Diner, a long-closed chain of beloved hot dog restaurants.

Staircases

Let's say you've made it to the top of the hill all on your own. Somehow you've held onto consciousness and you stand in awe over the city, the lack of oxygen adding an air of exhilaration to the experience. You catch your breath and take it all in, proud that you made it up here, to such a beautiful place, even if you had to abandon several of your friends in the process.

Eventually your mind will start to wander. Your attention drifts from the scenery to your stomach. This hike has completely depleted your energy. You need a burrito. You need to walk back downhill.

That's when you realize the only thing worse than walking up one of San Francisco's hills is walking down. So much impact on your poor knees. So difficult to find a comfortable stride. "Maybe I can just sit and scoot down to the bottom," you think as you slowly accept your fate.

But then, out of the corner of your eye, you spot a railing that seems out of place. It doesn't seem to be attached to any particular property. You walk over to investigate and to your delight, you discover a MUNICIPAL STAIRCASE!

A set of stairs designed exclusively for people in your situation. A generous gift from the city that says:

We know this place is impossible to walk around. Sorry about that. Hope this helps.

P.S. We would have put in an escalator but, you know, we're outside.

San Francisco's staircases come in all shapes and sizes and are there to help you get up and down all kinds of hills.

There are fancy staircases like the Lyon Street Steps, which look as if they've come straight out of a French palace, flanked with perfectly executed landscaping and sculpture. It's almost a little too much for me. When I walk them, I always feel like I'm trespassing and about to be taken out by the palace guards.

There are rugged staircases like the ones that take you up to the summits of Corona Heights Park or Twin Peaks, made from railroad ties and dirt. Sure, they may get a little muddy, but they make you feel as if you're in the middle of a National Park instead of a big city. Just remember: if you're taking a date to either of these spots, make sure they're not wearing brand new shoes.

Sorry, Nina.

There are brutalist staircases like Monument Way. As you approach the steps from 17th Street, it looks as if you are about to enter an indifferent cement cube. For a brief moment, you trudge toward your destination with no hope of beauty in your future. But halfway up you realize that it's quite a nice staircase. And it takes you to the top of hilariously named Mount Olympus, which is possibly the least Olympian of San Francisco's mounts.

It's cute, though.

There are commuter staircases like the Vulcan Stairs which lead directly into the doorways of many residencies. This kind of staircase feels like a little neighborhood. Its inhabitants take pride in the fact that they have to park on the streets below and hike up with supplies.

There are epic staircases like the 16th Avenue Tiled Steps in the Sunset. It's a one-block climb with 163 steps, each covered with colorful mosaic work featuring the sea, the sky, and a whole bunch of other things the artists threw in when the sea and the sky weren't enough to fill 163 steps.

And there are outlier staircases like the curlicue inclined plane that takes you to the bridge over the southern end of Market Street. Just hop on, start walking in circles and you'll get there eventually if you don't get too dizzy and need a sit-down.

There are even a few municipal slides at the Esmeralda Steps and Seward Mini Park, because why would you walk down a hill when gravity could do all the work?

Whenever I find myself incapacitated at the top of a massive hill, I take comfort in the fact that I won't have to serpentine all the way back down. And I feel thankful that I live in such a considerate city.

the Fog

It'll happen without warning. You'll strut down the street in your favorite pair of sunglasses, enjoying the summertime majesty of San Francisco. You'll gaze up at the sky, wondering how it can be so perfectly blue.

Then a wisp of white will pass in front of your eyes.

You'll shrug it off, and instead wonder how the sky can be so *nearly* perfectly blue. Then another wisp. And another. And one more.

Then your field of vision is rampaged by a horde of wispiness. It's moving fast now. Almost violently. You run and cower under a nearby bus shelter, but it's no use.

This is the fog.

Within minutes, it will devour the city.

The fog comes and goes. That is, unless you're in the Outer Sunset or Richmond Districts, where the fog keeps its permanent residence for most of the year. Just when you think the weather is too good to be true, it rolls in to remind you that life isn't supposed to be easy. Things can get dark and send a chill up your spine, but you're strsong and you can handle it. Where do you think you are, Los Angeles?

Sometimes the fog feels like San Francisco's blanket. Something you can pull over your head when the rest of the world gets a little too scary. Something to block out the prying eyes. Something to mask the allure of LA's Glitz and NYC's Glamour and allow you to truly be here and truly be yourself.

When it's foggy, don't be afraid. Don't stay in and hide. Go out. Put on a pair of your fanciest shoes and go clip-clopping down the glistening sidewalks. Climb to the top of a nearby hill and watch that great gray billow crawl through the valleys below. Give it an encouraging wave, then walk back down.

Dip a toe into the fog. Then dive in. Be amongst it. Breathe it in.

Get lost in it.

Layers

I was supposed to meet my friend Mike at the movie theater at one o'clock in the afternoon. It was a beautiful day. A regular beautiful day for San Francisco. The fog was taking a break, the sun was working overtime, and a soft breeze made for totally bearable tee shirt weather. The spring in my step bumped my ETA up to a quarter to one. I was early.

I took a seat on a stone wall near the entrance to the theater. I was in the shade. That's when I got cold. I went into my backpack, found a sweatshirt and threw it on. I looked at the clock. Mike wouldn't show up for another ten minutes. Luckily, this movie theater was the Kabuki on Post Street, which meant I was sitting in the heart of Japantown and a Japanese street festival just so happened to be in full swing. I stood up and got moving.

But as I walked out of the shadow and into the street, it was immediately too hot for a sweatshirt.

I walked back into the shadow. Perfect. Back into the street. Intolerable.

This isn't a gigantic city, but its geography and topography make for some weird little weather systems. Pockets of hot or cold or windy or showers that seem to come out of nowhere. If you look at the San Francisco weather and see one forecast, don't believe it. There should be a minimum of one forecast for every neighborhood. Good luck counting; a new little neighborhood pops up every day.

For the first time, I found myself between two of these microclimates. And the difference between them could be measured in sweatshirts. Well, one sweatshirt actually. One degree Sweatshirt.

Let's talk about layers.

You need them.

If you think you can roll out of the house in a tee shirt and return home that night after a day of perfect comfort, you are mistaken. Everyone in this city is walking around with a backpack for a reason. It's because dressing isn't something that happens in the morning here. It's something that continues to happen all day long.

It's alternating between short sleeves, long sleeves, rolled sleeves, cardigans, chore coats, windbreakers, and the obligatory puffer jacket. Every day in San Francisco ends with a puffer jacket.

You'll make mistakes. You'll think it's so beautiful outside you couldn't possibly need to pack a sweater. You just don't want to carry it. You want to be free and in the sun without a care in the world. Five hours later, you will find yourself miles away from that sweater, at the top of some hill in the shadow of some lonely raincloud, shivering and wondering how fast you can get to Chinatown so you can pick up a bootleg hoodie.

You'll promise to never leave the house without a few extra layers again. But soon there will be another beautiful day and you'll end up frozen in a mean little microclimate once again.

Try not to be too hard on yourself. It happens to the best of us.

It's 75°F and this person will **NOT BE** _OVERDRESSED_ in 10 minutes.

Smells

Every city has its smell. An aroma that defines your local olfactory experience.

For me, Portland is roasting coffee beans among the pines, New York is the sweet mustiness of summer in the subway, and Shanghai is just a wall of stinky tofu.

But San Francisco's particular bouquet is many things. It's layered like a fine wine or an above-average bean dip.

At its base, there's a strong presence of eucalyptus wafting with every gust of wind from Mount Sutro, Golden Gate Park, the Presidio, and pretty much everywhere else.

Next are the blossoms. One day, you'll walk down the street, find yourself under the right kind of tree and BAM! You are in a dreamy floral wonderland. You'll hover there with your eyes closed and a smile on your face, eliciting stares and scoffs from passersby. Don't feel self-conscious, they probably have sinus issues. The joke's on them.

After the blossoms have faded, the city throws in a

dash of sagebrush and a soupçon of wild fennel.

Then it's time for the real stars of the show.

Pee and weed.

The dynamic duo. A sign that, even though this city has changed considerably, it's still down to get weird regardless of the presence of a restroom. It's still down to throw on a faded Grateful Dead tee shirt and fall asleep on a park bench for a while.

Just when I think San Francisco has transformed into the interior of a Crate & Barrel, I turn a corner and I'm nostril-deep in ammonia and skunk.

That's when I know things are going to be all right.

the Flag

We all know of the Castro District as the capital of LGBTQ+ activism in San Francisco, if not the entire country. This is of course where Harvey Milk opened his legendary camera shop. The shop that later turned into his campaign headquarters where he'd become the first openly gay elected official in the state of California.

Today, the neighborhood remains proud of its groundbreaking history and this pride shows every day. So much so, you know when you've arrived at Castro Street before you even look up at a street sign. Because you will be surrounded by rainbow flags.

They're on light poles, they're in shop windows, and there are even rainbow crosswalks at the corner of Castro and 18th. But if you really want to feel the pride, walk two blocks north to Castro and Market. There, in the middle of Harvey Milk Square, you will find a flag pole with a gigantic rainbow flag.

In scale and color alone, it is breathtaking. It's so big, you can see it from places where you really shouldn't have a view of the Castro. And it is on a collision course with the wind that rolls down from Twin Peaks, so it is in constant, otherworldy motion. It sways and rolls like no other flag can. If you stare too long, it's mesmerizing. Sometimes when I'm driving at night and I hit the stoplight at Castro, I look up and see it illuminated, still rising and falling, lulling me into a state of hypnosis. The driver behind me always has to honk so I can come back to reality.

It is colossal, but even more so when you feel the history and love behind it. After all, it was Harvey Milk that asked his friend Gilbert Baker to design a symbol that they could rally behind. And it made its debut parading down Market Street in 1978.

Since then, rainbow flags have traveled the world fighting loud and proud for tolerance and acceptance.

But nowhere louder and prouder than in their home.

Just in case the pride flags weren't enough to let you know you're in the Castro, they went ahead and spelled it out for you on the side of a building.

This is the Castro Theatre. It's been around for over a century. Today, it's a repertory theater that usually puts on a new double feature every few days.

But it is also home to a perfect San Francisco moment. And it happens most every night of the week.

Show up early, grab a soda, popcorn, and a box of frozen Junior Mints. Then go into the theater and wait for the show to begin.

Twenty or thirty minutes before showtime, an organ quietly rises out of the stage. A gentleman with a big smile walks down the aisle and sits on the bench. Go ahead and give him a round of applause.

When he begins to play, the music may be related to the movie you're about to see. Or maybe it's just something that was in his head that day. Whatever it is, it will be delightful. Enjoy it as the room fills around you.

At about two minutes to showtime, it happens. The lights dim. The song he's playing fades away and in its place, you will hear the driving melody of "Theme from San Francisco."

Trust me, you've heard it before. It's the one that goes like this:

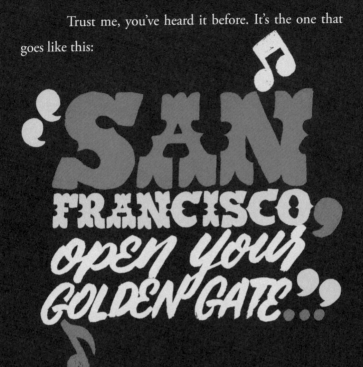

"'SAN FRANCISCO, open your GOLDEN GATE...'"

All of a sudden, everyone around you is clapping along. They've all been waiting for this. As the organ player goes into the song's bridge and the audience can no longer pretend that they know the words, take time to reflect on how wonderful a moment this is. Unadulterated civic pride.

This song was written for a movie called *San Francisco* starring Clark Gable and Jeanette MacDonald. It hasn't stuck around, but the song has. It's stuck around like anything written about a place that isn't used to having things written about it. Like "I Left My Heart in San Francisco." If that song were about New York City, it would have disappeared years ago. But it wasn't. It was written about San Francisco, so obviously this city has a statue of Tony Bennett.

The bridge leads into one final chorus and the clapping gets louder and louder as the gentleman plays the final notes. He stands to uproarious applause and waves as he walks away, and the organ sinks back below the stage. Everybody is primed for a phenomenal cinematic experience as the projector starts up.

What if you miss it? What if you walk into the theater late to an opening credit sequence?

Don't worry, it'll happen one more time before the second show.

Ocean Beach

Where San Francisco ends and the Pacific Ocean begins, there's a beach.

It's a wide beach with angry little waves and an overly serious undertow. It runs north to south along the Outer Richmond and the Outer Sunset with Golden Gate Park tucked in the middle.

Most of the time, the beach is covered with wind and clouds. Its beauty is stark and almost unwelcoming. Sometimes it's sunny, but the degree of starkness barely dips below surface-of-the-moon levels.

This beach isn't really for laying out. It's for having a sit-down with a friendly dog and a nice cup of coffee. It's an introspective place. I would say it's a good place to read a sad book, but the wind will refuse to keep you on one page for more than five seconds. I've tried.

To the north, you'll find the legendary Cliff House, which is actually the third or fifth Cliff House depending on who you ask. A San Francisco staple, this house is no stranger to fire and dynamite. It keeps getting knocked down and rebuilt. Each time a little stronger and more sensibly than before.

If you turn to the east, you'll see two gigantic, turn-of-the-last-century windmills standing guard over the trees of the park. Maybe you'll ask yourself, "Did the Dutch colonize San Francisco?" No, they didn't. The city just needed some water pumped.

But for me, the strangest and most interesting thing about this place filled with strange and interesting things is its name: *Ocean Beach*.

Yes. Yes it is an ocean beach. Did they think we'd mistake the Pacific Ocean for a lake? A very wide river?

"Which beach is it?"

"Ocean Beach."

"I know it's the ocean, I'm askin' ya the name of the beach"

"I'm tellin' ya, Ocean Beach."

"Oh boy."

FORT Funston

At the end of the Great Highway, just south of Ocean Beach and west of Lake Merced, is a piece of land called Fort Funston.

For a long time, it was one of the many places the Army put their really big guns to protect San Francisco's harbors. After a few decades of sitting around with nothing to do, the Army packed up their really big guns and moved on to more exciting theaters of war, eventually leaving the area in the capable hands of the National Park Service.

As you make your way up the sandy steps to the entrance, you may notice the city noise dying away, replaced with the sound of the ocean breeze through almost horizontal trees, tired after years of arguing with the wind. You may notice the stark, quiet landscape of golden dunes meeting a cool, gray sky at the edge of a cliff.

But the first thing you'll notice is that the entire place is made of sand and your choice of footwear is completely inappropriate, no matter what is on your feet. And you'll know that whatever awaits you on this journey into nature, you'll end up sitting on your bumper, slapping your shoes together, because you are not emotionally prepared to vacuum the car this weekend.

A hike in Fort Funston is more an expedition across an alien planet than a walk in the park. The south end features a launch for hang gliders. The sky is full of giant, mechanical birds. Scattered among the dunes are circular ruins. An armada of ancient spacecraft that landed on earth millennia ago, their pilots nowhere to be found. Look over the edge of the cliff and you'll see one embedded in the beach below. A crash landing. Or maybe just an old army bunker taken by erosion, once the post of many brave but incredibly bored soldiers.

But the real reason Fort Funston feels like a different world is because dogs are allowed to go off-leash. This is where every dog walker in the city comes to socialize their pups. For a few hours each day, Fort Funston becomes a planet of the dogs. Walk in and you will be surrounded. You will realize that they are the true rulers of this hunk of rock. They only allow you to be here out of the goodness of their gracious canine hearts.

It is a truly humbling experience. A reminder that these creatures we invite into our lives are wild. They long for power just like us. And maybe one day, they'll decided they don't want to sit and roll over anymore. Just in case, we should all show our allegiance to these puppy tyrants while there's still time.

All hail the dogs of Fort Funston. May your reign last seven-times-a-thousand years. And may your bellies forever be full of treats.

Line Culture

Go for a walk down any shop-lined street and eventually you'll see a parade of hungry, patient patrons flowing into a local establishment, just waiting to sink their teeth into *the* thing.

San Francisco has a lot of *the* thing.

It has *the* ice cream, *the* coffee, *the* toast, *the* ramen, *the* brunch, *the* egg tart, *the* croissant, *the* bubble tea, *the* morning bun, and *the* dim sum, just to name a few.

These "*the* things" begin life as very good things. They are so good that too many people want to experience them. An orderly line naturally forms as customers wait for their chance. Then those customers tell their friends how incredible *the* thing was. But more importantly, they tell them how long the line was. Their friends don't want to miss out, so the line gets longer, and then there are ropes and rules for the line, and all of a sudden it's no longer about *the* thing.

It's about the line.

Waiting in line has become a major pastime for San Francisco. When you think about it, if you give into the experience and don't focus on the fact that you want *the* thing and yet don't have *the* thing, it becomes a nice time spent with friends in the sunshine. Of course, you could just do that in a park or on a hike, but why not set yourself up for a nice treat at the end?

Don't get me wrong, I do think good things are worth waiting for, but I have trouble waiting in lines.

That's why if I'm in the mood for one of *the* things, I arrive ten minutes before they open, then waltz through the door.

Maybe that means I'm eating *the* bowl of ramen at ten thirty in the morning, but that's just fine with me.

These streets are a battlefield.

Too many people have too many cars and it seems that they all want to stop moving at the same time.

At every turn, you'll come face to face with a different set of hazard lights. Their owners have given up looking and if you want to continue, you'll have to play a game of chicken with whoever is coming down the other lane.

Double parking is a popular option. You could also try to find a lot. Or try to find a spot at the top of the nearest hill. Most people would rather abandon their car than climb back up.

Whatever you do, just don't try to park in front of somebody's garage. If you do, you'll have a whole heap of vigilante justice on your hands.

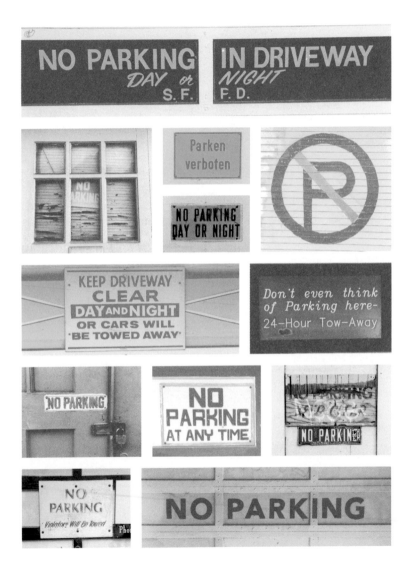

San Francisco Confetti

As I sit down to write this book, the very favorite activity of San Francisco's petty criminals is smashing car windows and taking everything inside. It's the perfect crime: pretty quick, no special tools required, and little chance of confrontation.

I've had more than a few friends lose laptops, phones, etc. One day I helped a family of German tourists search through the brush of Twin Peaks for their stolen passports. The police told them that these criminals aren't usually looking for documents and tend to throw them out the window as they speed away. Not this time, though. The family walked away empty-handed, unsure of how they would get home.

It's not unusual to see cars parked on the street with signs reading "nothing in car" taped to every single smashable window.

Before I continue, I'd just like to say that I think this is a bad thing. I wish people wouldn't smash car windows. At the very least it's incredibly annoying and at the worst it can really screw up someone's life.

However, this dumb crime wave has transformed the city into an art installation.

Everywhere you look, the ground is sparkling. All those tiny facets of safety glass catch the sunlight and become a giant, deconstructed, urban disco ball. And because almost all car windows are tinted, the sparkles come in different colors. Sometimes blue, but mostly green, adding to the city's natural motif.

Today, in most neighborhoods, this city can seem completely grit-free. Sometimes it feels like a grown-up amusement park. But San Francisco was born out of the Gold Rush. It used to be the Wild West. It was hard-drinkin' and -cussin' and -fightin'. Now that there's a yoga studio on every block, the city has chilled out, but sometimes it's good to feel that old hustle.

San Francisco's confetti keeps us on our toes both figuratively and literally.

Cable Cars

When I was nineteen I lived in Boston near the Park Street T stop. At that time, you could find plaques along the platform detailing the history of the city's public transportation. There was one image that always stood out to me. It was an illustration of a subway car around the turn of the twentieth century, riding along the same tunnel I traveled every day. But this subway car was different from the one I was about to board. This subway car had no sides. The passengers were hanging out all over the place. There was absolutely nothing to protect them from the rock wall of the tunnel as they sped past.

And I thought, "Now that's freedom."

The freedom to feel the wind in your hair. The freedom to reach out and interact with the world in a whole new way. The freedom to cause serious bodily harm oneself via public transportation.

I thought that freedom had been lost to history. Then I moved to San Francisco.

The cable cars are one of this city's most iconic attractions. Their 1870s style brings a sense of class and whimsy to San Francisco's ever-modernizing streets. Anyone can quite literally hop on and be whisked up and over the hills to the ding-ding of the bell and the dull grind of that massive cable making its way under the streets. Sit on the benches facing outward and watch the city pass by. Or if it's crowded, hang on to a railing and swing your body out into oncoming traffic. Go ahead, test fate, you're on vacation!

And I know you're on vacation because as I'm writing this, the price of a cable car fare is seven dollars. What daily commuter in their right mind would be willing to take on that expense?

But on a death-defying special occasion, it is well worth it.

the Buffalo

I guess outside of Yellowstone, I've never been in a place where it was reasonable to expect to see a buffalo. And a buffalo had never popped out and said hello as I rode my bike down the street. Until I moved to San Francisco.

In the middle of Golden Gate Park, there is a paddock filled with buffalo.

Bison, actually. American bison. But the paddock is called the Buffalo Paddock. So please just make of that what you will.

The herd began at the turn of the last century. A reminder of what the American West used to be. That's how they did nostalgia back then. Can a person be nostalgic for a time when nostalgia was still good?

Today, they say the herd remains as a nod to the park's history, but it's really there to baffle you. To add a little cognitive dissonance to your day. To rearrange your reality when you least expect it. It's there to make you ask:

"Have I finally discovered the ever elusive secrets of time travel!?"

Or at the very least:

"Why would anyone think to house a herd of bison in a major metropolitan area?"

Both are great questions.

Lombard vs. Vermont

For most of its length, Lombard is just your average street. It's flat, it's wide, and as part of U.S. Route 101, it helps get you where you need to go.

But if you're heading east and pass Hyde Street, things get different. As you go over the hill, you'll find that Lombard Street features eight crazy turns that guide drivers safely down the steep slope to Leavenworth Street. It is a feat of automotive choreography. Watching that steady stream of cars slowly flow down the hill can be hypnotic.

If these cars had anywhere to get to, they would have taken any other street. But they don't. They are simply there to have the Lombard Street experience. The city's tourists show up en masse to see it. It's just a quick walk from Fisherman's Wharf, after all. And it's right in the heart of San Francisco's upscale Russian Hill neighborhood. Lombard Street's perfect and colorful landscaping will make for an incredible photo. Just imagine their friends' envy when they learn that someone they know has visited *THE CROOKEDEST STREET IN THE WORLD*!

There's just one problem with this charmingly touristy scenario:

Lombard isn't the crookedest street in the world.

Three miles away, in a not-quite-as-posh neighborhood with just south of perfect landscaping, you'll find a stretch of Vermont Street between 22nd and 24th.

Sure, it may only have seven turns instead of Lombard's eight, but those seven turns swing wider than Lombard's. Some might even say they are "crookeder."

I would say that.

But Vermont Street doesn't draw attention to itself. It doesn't need the glory. It sits humbly by a public park, hiding in the shadows of nearby trees and the homes of Potrero Hill, almost unphotographable.

What a great attitude.

I respectfully ask Lombard Street to get over itself.

Sutro Tower

When you picture the landmarks of San Francisco you might think about the Golden Gate Bridge or Lombard Street, Coit Tower or the Painted Ladies. Or maybe just a big loaf of sourdough. These things are iconic. Their beauty and quirkiness represent their city perfectly.

But there's one landmark you'll leave out. One that quite literally towers over all the others.

Not only is Sutro Tower one of the tallest structures in San Francisco at 977 feet, it sits between Twin Peaks and Mount Sutro, two of the tallest peaks in the city. It's up there. You can see it from most of the city, which cannot be said of any other landmark. If you ever get lost, all you have to do is look up, find the tower, and you'll know exactly where you're going. If you're at the top of a mountain anywhere in the Bay Area, you'll see it standing proud and stealing attention from that tiny little Transamerica Building and the pebble they call Alcatraz.

So why isn't Sutro Tower one of the most recognizable features in the San Francisco skyline?

Maybe it hasn't had enough time to grow on the city. After all, it was only completed in 1973, a full forty years after the Golden Gate. Maybe the locals are just too busy looking out at that beautiful bay to turn around and give the tower the respect it deserves. Or maybe there's a simpler answer: it ain't cute.

Sutro Tower looks like the world's largest backyard drying rack.

It looks like something you stick into an ear of corn so you don't burn your fingers.

It looks like the arm of a giant evil robot emerging from the earth's core to destroy humanity.

It just looks weird.

But before 1973, TV and radio signals had a hard time maneuvering around San Francisco's hills and valleys. When the tower went up, the city lost its perfectly picturesque skyline and gained a beautiful new thing called good reception. That's a tough trade, but it was one the city was willing to make.

Decades later, the concept of good reception feels like a hilarious joke the past once played on us, but the tower is still there. Maybe it's not pretty enough to be appreciated by tourists, but for the city, it has become part of the landscape. After a long day, when you look up and see its prongs, tines, pointy parts, or whatever you call those things sticking out of the evening fog, you'll know that you are home.

Let the tourists keep the Golden Gate. Sutro Tower is for San Francisco.

Fisherman's Wharf

At one time, Fisherman's Wharf probably did a lot to define the vibe of San Francisco. A plate of fish and chips with a side of seabreeze, lit by the reds and blues of neon signs reflecting on the water.

But today, it's crowds, attractions, and kitschy souvenir shops.

If that's what you're into, fine. But I believe that the greatest possible moment of joy at Fisherman's Wharf is felt by a seagull when an uneaten, once chowder-filled bread bowl doesn't quite make it to the garbage can.

Fleet Week

It's Saturday morning. You lie awake listening to the chatter of the birds perched on the antenna outside your window and smelling the sweetness of a late summer bloom on the breeze. You smile as you realize you have nothing to do but enjoy life in this incredible city.

Then the world ends.

Your heart jumps out of your chest as a soul-shattering roar comes through the window. You jump out of bed, preparing to duck and cover before you look outside and see the Blue Angels happily cruising over the neighborhood. You breathe a sigh of relief as you realize that today isn't your day to die, it just happens to be Fleet Week.

Most of the roving bands of seamen tend to stay in and around North Beach and Downtown, so you might not see much of them, but those Blue Angels are impossible to ignore. They're out all weekend doing tricks and delighting the people of San Francisco. Well, at least delighting some people.

Others may think, "Hey, I love a barrel roll as much as the next bystander, but is it really a great idea to fly a fifty-million-dollar piece of hardware loaded with jet fuel over a major metropolitan area?"

I'll be honest: I've thought that. But then I thought, "You know what? What these pilots are doing is impressive and I can hear cheers and applause all over the city, so I'm just going to keep my worries to myself and try to enjoy."

Watching these planes fly across the city in a matter of seconds is incredible. It gives you a new perspective on this little peninsula. You'll experience a whole new sense of San Francisco's scale, which feels great even if you have to experience it while practicing deep breathing exercises.

Now on that magical day when a jet engine rips me out of my slumber, I simply cheer along with the rest of the city.

WOOOO! BE CAREFUL!

The probability is low that you, the person who is reading this book right now, are a nudist.

If you happen to be one, thanks for buying this book. I'm so happy you're here. But I have to let you know that the next two pages are not for you. You won't find this fun or surprising. It'll just be normal for you. But hang in there and I'll put something really fun on the next page.

For all you regular shame-filled humans out there, this one's for you. Gird your loins.

On my way home from Twin Peaks one day, I found myself walking down 19th Street just east of Castro. I came across a little side street and saw a man walking toward the corner. He wasn't wearing a shirt and his bottom half was covered by a row of parked cars. There was just something about his swagger. Something that told me this wasn't about to be an ordinary meeting of two people on a street corner. Something about the physics of his movement suggested that he was wearing unconventional bottoms. Perhaps a pair of Daisy Dukes or even a utilikilt.

But as he emerged from the cars, I realized that my instincts weren't exactly right.

Because in that moment I was looking him square in the penis.

My brain was sent hurtling into crisis mode, pulled itself together, and sent me this transmission:

Well, that's a wiener. Wieners are fine. This gentleman is living his life exactly the way he wants to and it has nothing to do with you. Just stare perfectly straight ahead and pretend everything is normal because you're cool and this isn't an issue for you.

Two seconds later, we passed and headed in different directions. My brain took a breather and prepared for the next exposed genital situation. Which, in this city, is always just around the corner.

It's never really a bad time to expose your genitals to the general public in San Francisco. It might be Pride weekend, it might be Halloween, or it might just be an especially lovely afternoon. Whatever the case, feel free to whip it out and do your thing. At any time of year, San Francisco's climate is ready to accept your tender parts with warm sunlight and a cool breeze. San Francisco's laws, however, aren't so welcoming.

Social nudity was made illegal in 2012. You can get a special nudity permit from the city but some nudists simply cover their bits with small satchels or loin cloths. Perhaps it's just a legal loophole, but I like to think it's also a courtesy to those of us brought up on the uptight East Coast. A way to save us some embarrassment, but also remind us that we aren't as free as we could be. Or maybe it's just a fun excuse to accessorize.

In any case, these options still allow the wearer to feel the breeze on his or her butt, which I think we can all agree is an underrated sensation.

There are two major highways that connect San Francisco to the north and the south: U.S. Route 101 and Interstate 280. But if you live in California and call them by their proper names, you're gonna get looked at funny. Here they are simply the 101 (One Oh One) and the 280 (Two Eighty).

The 101 is a helpful highway. It can take you down to the Peninsula and up to Marin County. But even though it's a north/south route, the 101 seems to flow upward from its southern terminus in Los Angeles. It's LA's highway. It has an LA attitude and it's not at all concerned with SF or its feelings. When it first arrived, it simply said:

Yo, I'm the 101. I'm one thousand five hundred and forty miles long and I'm kind of a big deal. SF, I'm gonna have to ask you to move aside because I'm from the second biggest city in America and what are you, the thirteenth biggest? That's cute, now please get out of my way because I have places to go.

Now, if there's one thing San Francisco can't stand, it's being made to feel like a second-class city. So when the 101 showed up, it responded:

Whoa, slow down there. We're sure you have a lot of 'really important' places to go, but this isn't LA. We do things differently here and honestly, we just don't have space for you. You're going to have to share. So just let's get rid off all these overpasses and get you down to street level. We have an incredible thoroughfare here called Van Ness Avenue. You're welcome to roll up there if you want to. It has a bunch of traffic lights and stop signs. We know highways aren't used to that kind of thing, but you're just going to have to deal with it.

Then go ahead and take a left on Lombard. Oh, you've never taken a left before? Well, there's a first time for everything. After that, maybe cruise through the Presidio, just one of our many massive parks. We're one of the greenest cities in America. Not a huge deal, but we're sure you don't know anything about that.

Finally, you can show yourself out of our beautiful

city by crossing one of the most beautiful and recognizable bridges in the world. It's called the Golden Gate, maybe you've heard of it. Then you're free to go about your business up north.

Bye! Don't let the Marin Headlands hit ya where the good lord split ya!

San Francisco continues to tolerate the 101, but this highway holds no place in its heart.

The 280 is a different story. It's only 57 miles long and seems to flow down from its northern terminus at 5th and King Street in San Francisco's SOMA neighborhood. It is one with the city and unlike the 101, the 280 waits for you with open arms. Even its on ramps are informal and easy to maneuver. As you set your wheels onto its surface it seems to say:

Oh, it's you! I'm so excited to see you. I'm goin' as far as San Jose and you're welcome to join me. But first, let's just look at this beautiful city together. All these buildings stacked on top of one another. I never get tired of it. Look, I know you're probably trying to get to one of the cities on the Peninsula, but if you don't mind, I'm gonna swerve a little west of them. I rather see trees than sprawl, you know? Oh, you agree? Great.

Let's cruise through these rollings hills for a while. Watch this, I'll take us into the clouds and then right back out again. Hey, do you like lakes? Look, it's the Lower Crystal Springs Reservoir. Pretty, right? Oh, you're ready to get off. Well, If you head east, you'll find some real nice Japanese food in San Mateo. And if you go west, you'll cruise right into Half Moon Bay. You could jump into the ocean if you wanted to, but it's super cold, so I wouldn't. It's been real nice driving with you. Seeya soon!

While the 101 wants to take you somewhere else, the 280 just wants to show you how beautiful the Bay really is. It's charming and it's local, which is what San Francisco is all about.

Those Weird
Brick Circles
in the Middle
of the Street

At first, you won't see them at all. Large brick circles embedded in the blacktop that make your tires buzz for a split second as you roll over the. Seems totally normal when your mind has other things going on. Just another road marker or a quick fix from the SFMTA.

But as you drive over them again and again, they become landmarks. You expect them. When you venture outside of your commute, you begin to see them elsewhere. Maybe you'll give them a fleeting thought. "There's another one of those brick circle things. Is it a motif? I don't quite get it, but that's San Francisco, I guess!"

As you explore and really get to know your way around the city, you'll see them everywhere. Then one day, you'll shout this to no one in particular:

Why are there giant circles of bricks all over the place!?

For me, it was three years from that point to the moment I finally searched for the answer. Somewhere in that time, I had convinced myself that they must be turnarounds for old streetcar lines. Sure, some of them don't quite match up perfectly with the city's grid system, but it's plausible enough and I have other stuff to wonder about, like, "The Salesforce tower looks really tall, will it ruin my chapter about how Sutro Tower is the tallest structure in San Francisco?"

The answer, as you've probably already read, is *yes*, very, very annoyingly.

One day, possibly several years later, you will have a clear enough head to notice these circles on your commute home and search for the answer as soon as you get through the door.

Then, at long last, you will discover that they are massive cisterns buried underground.

Actually, I guess you've just discovered that now. Sorry for spoiling the surprise. Unless you already knew. If you did, good for you! What a little beacon of civic pride you are!

These brick circles, which can be up to 32 feet in diameter, show us the whereabouts of 177 underground cisterns, built as an auxiliary water supply for the fire department after the earthquake of 1906. It seems as though the city wasn't too excited about burning to the ground again. Go figure.

Each cistern can hold between 75,000 and 200,000 gallons of water. Or any other liquid, I guess. I wonder if the city has explored other possibilities. Mimosa cisterns for epic emergency brunches? Anyway, because they are totally independent of the regular water supply, they can help out even if the entire system goes down.

But that hasn't happened in a long time. Just in case, I'm currently knocking on all kinds of wood.

Wood that probably won't be on fire anytime soon.

Thanks, cisterns.

Valencia and Mission

In the middle of the city, there is one block that is different from all others. It's a block that transports you into another dimension. Perhaps even another time stream. Nobody really knows for sure. We might need to do a little more research.

This is the block between Valencia Street and Mission Street. Actually, it's every block between Valencia and Mission.

It wasn't always like this, but some years ago that aloof weirdo named Gentrification came to town and said:

Mission Street, I like what you've got going on here. It's a little hectic, it's a little loud, it's a little dangerous. I need your energy to validate my street cred. Keep doing your thing. Valencia Street, I like you. You have potential. I see shops, I see baked goods, I see all kinds of fancy stuff.

Let's get down to business.

And now that one block is a gateway between cultural, aesthetic, and financial realities.

You can eat a meal at a Michelin-starred restaurant on Valencia, then walk a block to Mission and pick out a live fish at a Chinese wet market.

You can celebrate the Day of the Dead with thousands of humans on Mission, then walk a block to Valencia and drink a twelve-dollar cold-pressed juice completely alone.

You can purchase a taxidermied hippopotamus on Valencia, then walk one block and find five people on one street corner yelling about Jesus through amps that were not made to handle their level of passion.

That block is an interesting union of worlds, but also a humbling reminder that humans want to be near the real stuff. The authentic, the unfettered. And when people can't make the real stuff themselves, they'll pay a premium to be near other people's real stuff.

Then the real stuff gets priced out and all this city will have left is the cold comfort of some overpriced juice and a dead hippo.

the Palace of Fine Arts

Built for the 1915 Panama-Pacific Exposition, the Palace of Fine Arts is a beautiful piece of San Francisco's history. Its design is classical, its effect awe-inspiring, and it feels 100% out of place in a major U.S. metropolitan area.

On clear days, the sun turns the city's fire escapes into a modern art installation.

That One Sunset

Even the least interesting San Francisco sunsets are pretty good. When the sky is clear, you'll see a light wash of goldenrod over the City as the sun sinks behind the Golden Gate and into the Pacific Ocean.

When there are a few clouds hanging around, things start to get a little more interesting. They'll go from white to gold, then all the way to magenta over the course of twenty minutes.

Then there's that one sunset. It only happens a few times a year. The one that'll make you look up and think, "Is this the apocalypse? Oh man, I was just about to get an ice cream." The sky turns neon pink while the clouds border on electric purple. There might even be a splash of fire engine red in there.

If you see it, run outside. Because for the next five minutes, everything you look at will become the most beautiful version of itself.

There's something about that light. That deep, warm light makes the world a better place. The trees seem happier, the skyline is more heroic, and your loved ones are more attractive than you ever could have imagined.

When those five minutes are up, the light will fade and everything will go back to normal. The trees, buildings and people go back to being their perfectly lovely selves, but now in darkness.

But you will have changed. You will know just how good everything can be.

And every sunset until the next That One Sunset will just be a regular sunset.

Twin Peaks

Just west of a metal disc on the sidewalk signifying the geographic center of San Francisco sit two mounds of earth. I'd call them peaks, but to me the word peak denotes cragginess, snowiness, hard-to-get-to-iness. These are mounds. A pleasant pair of protuberances poking their heads out from the city's colorful duvet of houses and apartment buildings

When I first moved here, my friend Hélène took me on a drive around the city. When we cruised through the western slope of Eureka Valley, she pointed and said, "Twin Peaks." I told her I love *Twin Peaks*. Surprised that I had been there before, she started talking about how much she loves Twin Peaks. It took us a good two minutes before we realized that she was talking about Twin Peaks the place and I was talking about *Twin Peaks* the show. We both got a great recommendation that day.

Twin Peaks is the kind of place you look up at and think, "I wonder if I can get up there." But you don't have to wonder. Those charming little bumps are smiling down at you and yelling, "Come on up!" Then all you have to do is walk toward them.

The city has made sure that you will find your way. If you're coming from the east, a municipal staircase will lead you to a corkscrew walkway, which will take you over the tail end of Market Street, which leads to a path, which leads you to a nice dog that you can pet, which leads you to five more municipal staircases, which leads you to those steps made of old railroad ties that we talked about earlier, and those will take you to one of the two summits.

Welcome to Twin Peaks.

The type of magical experience you are about to undergo will be determined by the time of day and weather conditions upon your arrival.

On a cloudy day, as you climb the last set of steps to the summit, the city disappears. Sutro Tower disappears. The road below you disappears. And when you get to the top, the steps behind you disappear, leaving you in a room made of clouds. Everything is quiet. No one else will have braved the walk, so you will be in the room alone. Take a seat on the rocky floor. Bring a folding chair. This room will never exist again. It is yours. Bring a little table and eat a burrito. Bring a friend and some speakers and have a dance party in your room. It's up to you.

When the wind is just right, you may see a raven frozen in the sky. It takes off, finds some kind of equilibrium, and seems to hover in midair, flying and not flying at the same time.

If you had wings, you'd be up there too.

On a cloudy evening, the wind will try to keep you away. Halfway there, you'll turn down a street and find yourself in an aggressive weather system flowing downhill and rushing through the streets. It will fill your ears with overwhelming white noise. It will tell you to go drink hot chocolate instead of completing your journey, but you will fight your way up the steps and when you get to the top, the wind will take your breath away. If you could talk, no one would be able to hear you. Your eyes will tear up, your skin will ripple, and you'll think, "This is incredible, but the wind sure was right about that hot chocolate thing." You'll walk down triumphant and in search of cocoa.

On a clear day, San Francisco will lay itself out before you like a train set. You'll see the Golden Gate and the Marin Headlands to the north. You'll see Mount Diablo to the east and a whole lot of Pacific Ocean to the west. And you won't be alone. You'll be in a crowd with every tourist in the city. They'll be slower than you'll want them to be. Be patient, they're trying to chill out. They will be successful if you let them.

On a clear evening, Twin Peaks is at its best. Keep your eyes on the sun as it approaches the horizon and the sky burns orange. Turn around to fill your field of vision with pink and purple. The first porch lights appear on the skyline as the colors deepen and the sun sinks into the Pacific once more. The colors depart quickly, leaving the night to turn the city into a blanket of twinkling stars. Street lights, office lights, living room lights. Take them in. Try to snap a picture and fail to capture them.

Know that the only thing to do is to walk back down those steps and join them. Laugh with old friends under them. Make out with new friends under them. Walk too far up a too steep hill under them.

And know that you're home in this tiny, gigantic, booming, and quiet little city.

This is San Francisco.